Garden flowers
in cross-stitch

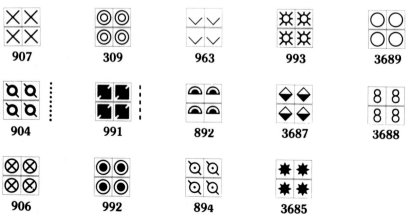

Clematis

907 309 963 993 3689

904 991 892 3687 3688

906 992 894 3685

Garden flowers
in cross-stitch

ZARZA

LE TEMPS APPRIVOISÉ
7, rue Abel Hovelacque
75013 PARIS

Zarza

Zarza graduated in 1972 from the French school of industrial design, the Ecole nationale des arts appliqués à l'industrie, then studied for two years at the major French art school, the Ecole des Beaux-Arts.

A lover of nature and the countryside, he soon became known for his original compositions (Salon des ateliers d'art Exhibition, 1985).

He loves to experiment and is as skilled in airbrushing as in painting on silk.

Embroidery photographs: Janine Sicart.

Computerised diagrams: Jean-Claude Moissinac for Daikiri.

DMC has very efficiently helped us with the realisation of the embroideries

© Pierre Zech Éditeur, Paris, 1989
ISBN 2.283.58084.6
Printed in Spain

Introduction

From painting to embroidery...

Nature will always be a privileged and inexhaustible supply of inspiration for all art forms. The trained eye of the painter never ceases to discover its wonders. That is why all the patterns presented in this booklet were originally created in gouache paint.

The fine detailing and richness of colour, drawing and composition are remarkably well-adapted to the cross-stitch technique. The artist himself chose the correct DMC threads from the vast range of colours to match the hues indicated for each plant.

The practical advice at the beginning, which should be read before you begin work, makes these patterns suitable for all levels of embroiderers despite their apparent complexity.

Before you begin

The materials

The patterns shown here should be embroidered on evenweave linen of 10.5 threads to the centimeter (about 26 to the inch). The designs should be embroidered using two strands of DMC Mouliné Special (Ref.: art. 117) and a blunt-ended tapestry needle (number 22 to 24). An embroidery hoop is very useful to keep the fabric taut.

Using the diagrams

Each cross-stitch corresponds to one square of the diagram and covers two weft and two warp threads. The size of the finished embroidery thus depends on the number of threads per centimeter of the fabric used.

The symbols below each diagram correspond to the colours of thread used in the pattern. The number accompanying each symbol refers to the DMC colour chart which you will find on pages 10 and 11.

Preparing your work

Before starting to embroider, oversew the fabric all round to prevent it from unravelling. Then mark it out with tacking stitch in coloured thread, 1 inch from the edges, covering 10 threads over and 10 threads under the fabric on at least two sides. This will eventually help you to count your stitches. Then count the number of threads lengthwise and crosswise, and mark the halfway point, horizontally and vertically, with a row of running stitches in coloured thread (10 threads over and 10 threads under). The point at which the threads cross will give you the centre point, which is indicated on the diagrams by two arrows. Pull the running stitch out when the embroidery is completed.

Embroidery

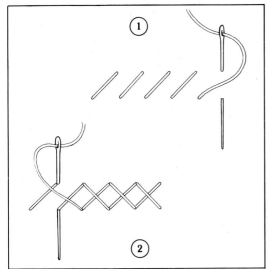

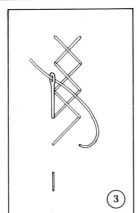

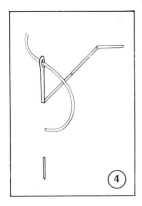

Cross-stitch

Each complete stitch consists of two diagnonals which cross in the centre. To make a row of stitches, sew a series of diagonals, each covering two threads of the fabric working form bottom to top and from left to right (1), then go back over the stitches, using another series of diagnonal stitches from right to left to cross over the previous series (2).

Begin at the top row.

To work vertically (3), each whole stitch must be completed separately. Sew a diagonal stitch from bottom to top and from left to right, then from right to left, bringing the needle out two threads below the stitch thus created, in order to begin the next one.

Whether you are working horizontally or vertically, all the stitches must cross in the same direction. It is also important for the neatness of the work not to pull the embroidery thread too tightly; the thread should cross two fabric threads without pulling them together.

Backstitch (4) is used for the stems. It forms a continuous line of short stitches which means you can follow curved lines. Insert the needle at the beginning of the line and bring it out a little further on. Bring the needle back and put it through the first hole, bringing it out a little further on, and so on.

Backstitch is shown on the diagrams by a full or dotted line repeated on the right of the symbol of the color to be used.

Try and avoid making knots when starting or finishing work. Leave a 1 1/5 inch (3 cm) end when you start the embroidery and hold it in place with subsequent stitches. To finish off or when a piece of thread is used up, slide the thread under the last stitches you made.

Needlework projects

The designs presented in the following pages will blend in beautifully with any colour scheme, thanks to their diversity of composition and colour. They will give your table linen an elegant, personalized note, or you can make them into various types of soft furnishings such as cushions, picture frames and so on.

Table runner (not shown)
Fabric size: 15 × 41 inches (37 × 102 cm).
Size of finished needlework: 14 × 40 inches (35 × 100 cm).
First, center the chosen design on the fabric (the center of the embroidery should be about 7 1/2 inches (18,5 cm) from the edge of the fabric) at each end of the table runner. Finish with a 1/5 inch (5 cm) wide open hem made by pulling out two threads right around the needlework 2/3 inch (1,5 cm) from the edge.

Table linen set (not shown)
Fabric size: 13 × 19 inches (32 × 47 cm).
Size of finished needlework: 12 × 18 inches (30 × 45 cm).
Proceed as for table runner.

Cushion
Fabric size: 17 × 34 1/2 inches (42 × 85 cm) for a 16 × 16 inches (40 × 40 cm) cushion.
Complete the embroidery, centering it on one half of the fabric. Assemble the cushion with backstitch, adding coloured piping if desired.

Framing
Fabric size: 18 × 18 inches (45 × 45 cm).
Frame the finished needlework with a passe-partout in a colour of your choice.

Needlework holder
Fabric size: 18 1/2 × 26 inches (46 × 65 cm).
Size of the finished holder: 18 × 12 inches (44 × 30 cm).
Center the design within a rectangle made from half of the fabric. When you have completed the embroidery, assemble the holder using backstitch and line it with cotton fabric. If you like, you can add a zip fastner to close it. Then sew on the handles.

TABLEAU DE RECHERCHE DES Nᵒˢ DE COULEURS
KEY TO COLOR NUMBERS
TABELLE ZUM AUFSUCHEN DER FARBNUMMERN
DMC KLEURENSCHEMA

Coul. Nᵒˢ / Color # / Kleuren Nrs / Farben	Col. Kolom	Coul. Nᵒˢ / Color # / Kleuren Nrs / Farben	Col. Kolom	Coul. Nᵒˢ / Color # / Kleuren Nrs / Farben	Col. Kolom	Coul. Nᵒˢ / Color # / Kleuren Nrs / Farben	Col. Kolom	Coul. Nᵒˢ / Color # / Kleuren Nrs / Farben	Col. Kolom	Coul. Nᵒˢ / Color # / Kleuren Nrs / Farben	Col. Kolom	Coul. Nᵒˢ / Color # / Kleuren Nrs / Farben	Col. Kolom
Couleurs Ombrées		+ 301	3	452	17	+ 666	5	+ 798	7	+ 913	6	+ 995	12
48	22	304	8	453	17	+ 676	14	+ 799	7	+ 915	7	+ 996	12
51	20	+ 307	5	+ 469	12	+ 677	14	+ 800	7	917	7	3011	14
52	21	+ 309	1	+ 470	12	680	14	+ 801	10	+ 918	11	3012	14
53	21	+ 310	8	+ 471	12	+ 699	8	+ 806	11	919	11	3013	14
57	20	311	3	+ 472	12	+ 700	8	+ 807	11	+ 920	11	3021	16
61	21	312	3	+ 498	8	+ 701	8	809	7	921	11	3022	16
62	22	315	13	500	15	+ 702	8	813	5	+ 922	11	3023	16
67	22	316	13	+ 501	15	+ 703	8	814	8	924	15	3024	16
69	20	317	12	+ 502	15	704	8	+ 815	8	926	15	3031	16
75	21	+ 318	12	503	15	+ 712	3	816	8	927	15	3032	16
90	20	319	1	+ 504	15	+ 718	7	817	5	928	15	3033	16
91	21	+ 320	1	517	10	720	18	+ 818	1	+ 930	4	3041	16
92	20	+ 321	8	+ 518	10	721	18	819	1	931	4	3042	16
93	20	+ 322	3	+ 519	10	722	18	820	7	+ 932	4	+ 3045	13
94	21	326	1	520	18	+ 725	7	+ 822	2	934	15	+ 3046	13
95	20	327	16	522	18	+ 726	7	+ 823	3	935	12	3047	13
99	21	333	18	523	18	+ 727	7	824	5	936	15	3051	15
101	21	334	3	524	18	+ 729	14	825	5	+ 937	12	3052	15
102	21	335	1	535	12	+ 730	14	+ 826	5	+ 938	10	3053	15
103	20	+ 336	3	543	13	731	14	+ 827	5	939	3	3064	13
104	22	340	18	550	8	+ 732	14	+ 828	5	+ 943	10	3072	17
105	20	341	18	+ 552	8	733	14	+ 829	14	+ 945	9	3078	13
106	21	347	11	+ 553	8	+ 734	14	830	14	946	1	+ 3325	3
107	21	+ 349	5	+ 554	8	+ 738	10	831	14	+ 947	1	3326	1
108	20	350	5	561	18	+ 739	10	+ 832	14	+ 948	5	3328	11
111	22	+ 351	5	562	18	+ 740	2	833	14	+ 950	13	3340	19
112	22	+ 352	5	563	18	741	2	+ 834	14	+ 951	13	3341	19
113	20	+ 353	5	564	18	+ 742	2	+ 838	6	954	6	+ 3345	9
114	22	355	9	+ 580	11	743	2	839	6	+ 955	6	3346	9
115	22	+ 356	9	+ 581	11	+ 744	2	+ 840	6	+ 956	10	+ 3347	9
116	22	367	1	+ 597	15	+ 745	2	+ 841	6	+ 957	10	+ 3348	9
121	22	+ 368	1	+ 598	15	746	13	+ 842	6	958	19	3350	4
122	22	369	1	600	6	+ 747	10	844	16	959	19	3354	4
123	22	370	18	+ 601	6	+ 754	5	869	15	961	4	3362	19
124	21	371	18	602	6	+ 758	9	+ 890	1	962	4	3363	19
125	20	372	18	+ 603	6	760	11	891	2	963	4	3364	19
126	22	400	3	604	6	761	11	+ 892	2	964	19	3371	10
		+ 402	3	+ 605	6	+ 762	12	893	2	966	7	3607	19
Couleurs Unies,		+ 407	13	+ 606	4	772	18	+ 894	2	970	9	3608	19
Tapisserie et		+ 413	12	+ 608	4	775	3	895	9	+ 971	9	3609	19
Nouv. Coloris		+ 414	12	610	16	+ 776	1	+ 898	10	+ 972	9	+ 3685	4
‡*Bl. Neige	1	+ 415	12	611	16	778	13	+ 899	1	+ 973	9	+ 3687	4
‡*Ecru	11	420	15	612	16	+ 780	7	+ 900	1	+ 975	12	3688	4
+ 208	2	422	11	613	9	781	7	+ 902	8	+ 976	12	+ 3689	4
209	2	+ 433	10	632	13	+ 782	7	+ 904	4	+ 977	12	3705	19
+ 210	2	+ 434	10	‡*640	2	+ 783	7	+ 905	4	986	3	3706	19
+ 211	2	435	10	‡*642	2	791	9	906	4	+ 987	3	3708	19
221	13	+ 436	10	‡*644	2	792	9	+ 907	4	988	3		
223	13	+ 437	10	645	16	793	9	+ 909	6	+ 989	3		
224	13	+ 444	5	646	16	794	9	910	6	+ 991	11		
225	13	+ 445	5	647	16	+ 796	7	+ 911	6	992	11		
+ 300	3	451	17	648	16	+ 797	7	912	6	+ 993	11		

DMC COLOR CHART
(Art. 117-115-116)

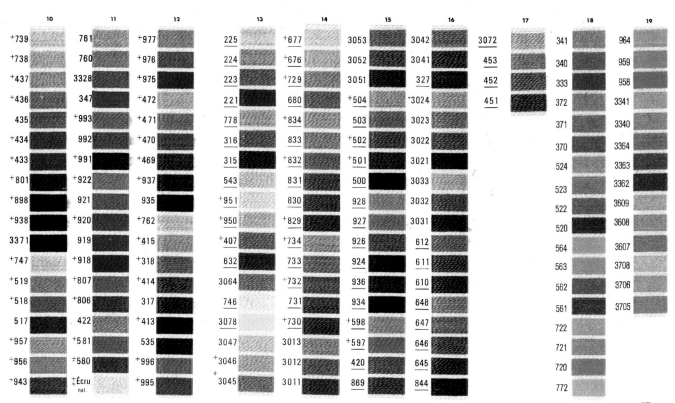

1	2	3	4	5	6	7	8	9
+BLANC Neige	+745	775	+3689	+948	+955	+800	+321	+758
819	+744	+3325	3688	+754	954	809	304	+356
+818	743	334	+3687	+353	+913	+799	+498	355
+776	+742	+322	+3685	352	912	+798	816	+3348
3326	741	312	+907	+351	+911	+797	+815	+3347
+899	+740	311	906	350	910	+796	814	3346
335	+211	+336	+905	+349	+909	820	+902	+3345
+309	+210	+823	+904	817	+842	+727	704	895
326	209	939	+608	+828	+841	+726	+703	+973
369	+208	+402	+606	+827	+840	+725	+702	+972
+368	+822	+301	963	813	839	+783	+701	+971
+320	+644	400	962	+826	+838	+782	+700	970
367	+642	+300	961	825	+605	781	+699	613
319	+640	+989	+932	824	604	+780	+554	794
+890	+894	988	931	+445	+603	966	+553	793
+947	893	+987	+930	+307	602	+718	+552	792
946	+892	986	3354	+444	+601	917	550	791
+900	891	+712	3350	+666	600	+915	+310	+945

10	11	12	13	14	15	16	17	18	19
+739	761	+977	225	+677	3053	3042	3072	341	964
+738	760	+976	224	+676	3052	3041	453	340	959
+437	3328	+975	223	+729	3051	327	452	333	958
+436	347	+472	221	680	+504	3024	451	372	3341
435	+993	+471	778	+834	503	3023		371	3340
+434	992	+470	316	833	+502	3022		370	3364
+433	+991	+469	315	+832	+501	3021		524	3363
+801	+922	+937	543	831	500	3033		523	3362
+898	921	935	+951	830	928	3032		522	3609
+938	+920	+762	+950	+829	927	3031		520	3608
3371	919	+415	+407	+734	926	612		564	3607
+747	+918	+318	632	733	924	611		563	3708
+519	+807	+414	3064	+732	936	610		562	3706
+518	+806	317	746	731	934	648		561	3705
517	422	+413	3078	+730	+598	647		722	
+957	+581	535	3047	3013	+597	646		721	
+956	+580	+996	+3046	3012	420	645		720	
+943	+Écru nat.	+995	+3045	3011	869	844		772	

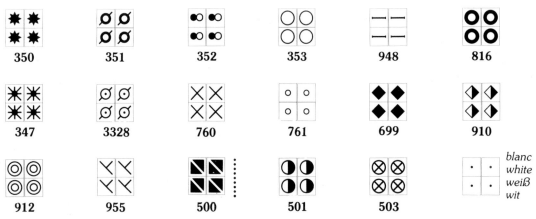

350   351   352   353   948   816

347   3328   760   761   699   910

912   955   500   501   503   *blanc*
white
weiß
wit

Dipladenia

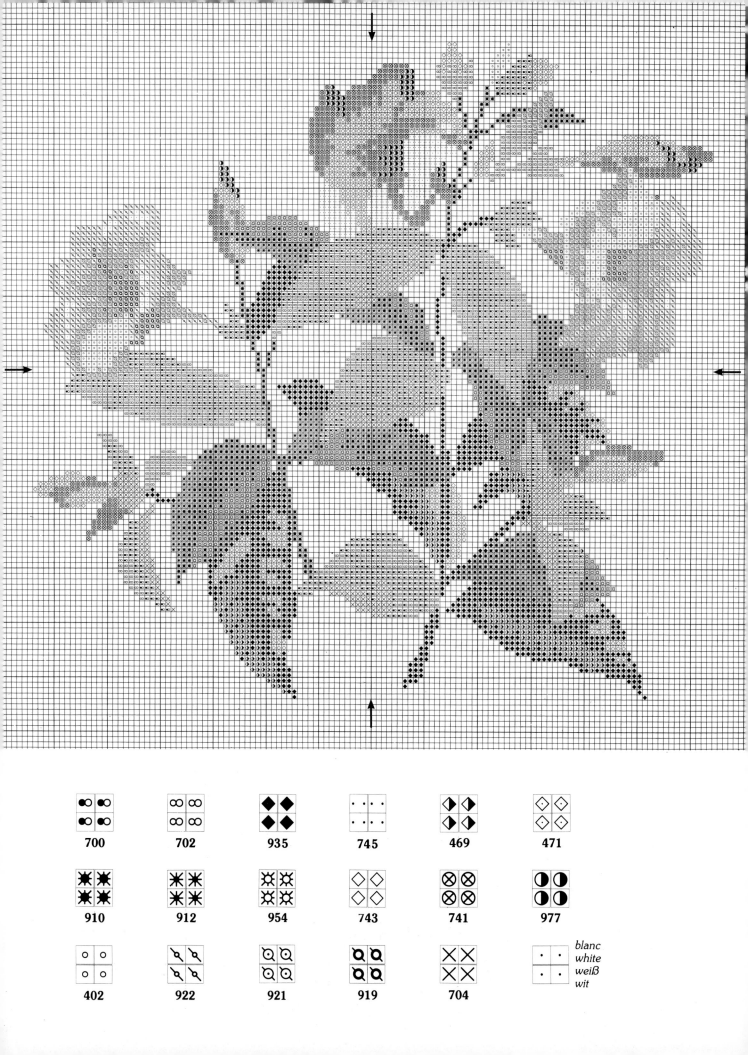

700 702 935 745 469 471

910 912 954 743 741 977

402 922 921 919 704

blanc
white
weiß
wit

Allamanda

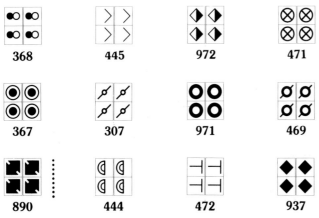

368   445   972   471

367   307   971   469

890   444   472   937

Redoutea

Redutea heterophylla

312   955   911   725   554

336   913   727   552

939   909   726   550

Pansy

Viola wittrockiana

19

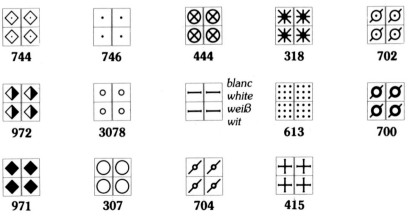

744 **746** **444** **318** **702**

972 **3078** blanc / white / weiß / wit **613** **700**

971 **307** **704** **415**

Narcissus

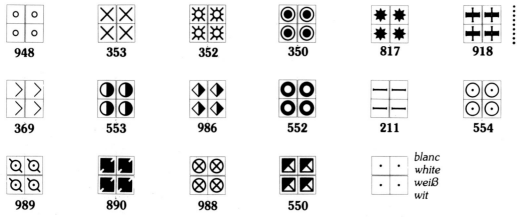

948 · 353 · 352 · 350 · 817 · 918

369 · 553 · 986 · 552 · 211 · 554

989 · 890 · 988 · 550

blanc
white
weiß
wit

Petunia

Petunia hybrida

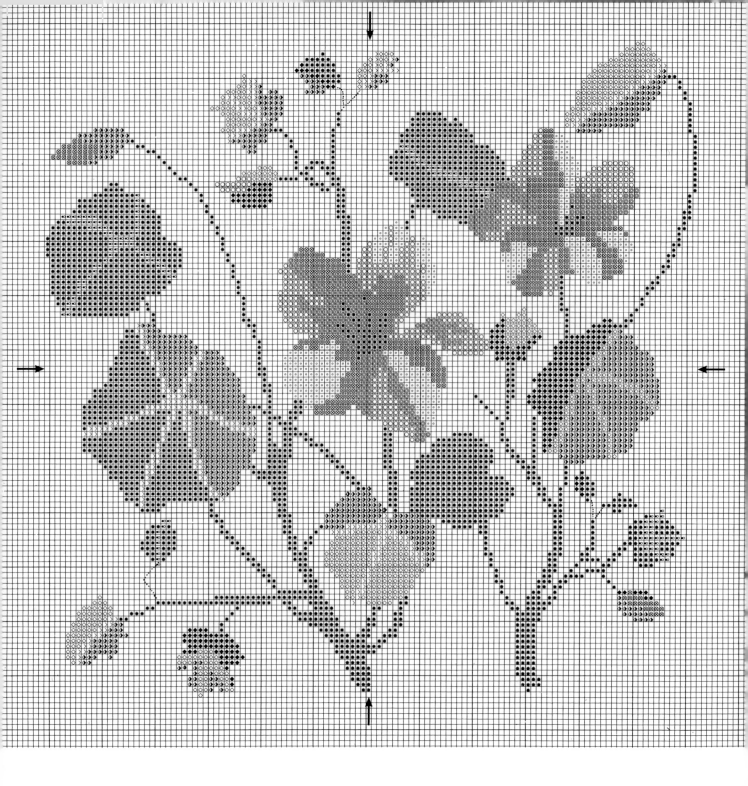

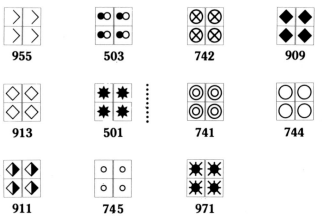

955   503   742   909

913   501   741   744

911   745   971

Nasturtium

Troppaeolum majus

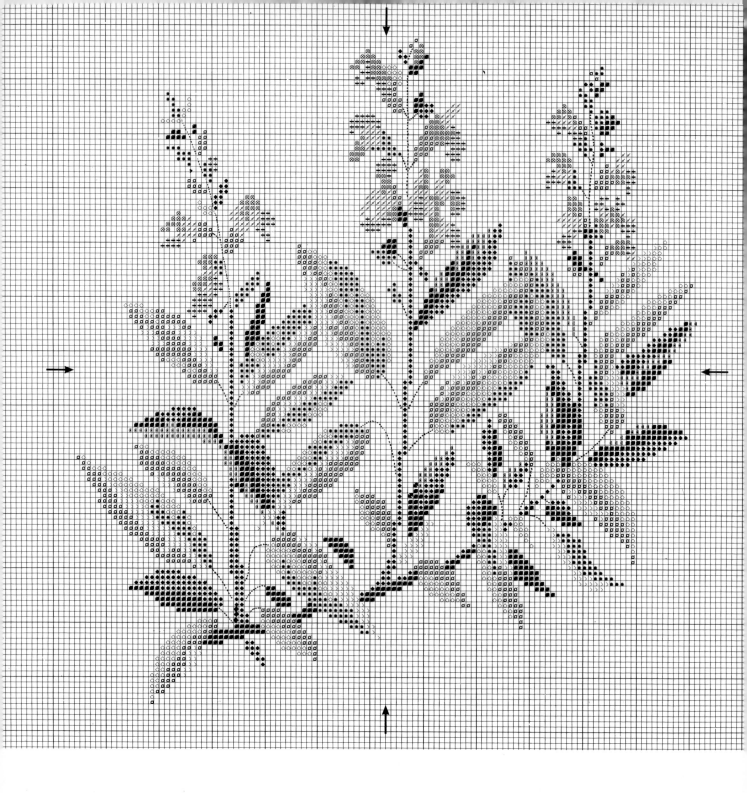

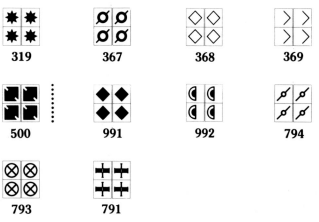

✴✴ ✴✴	✍✍ ✍✍	◇◇ ◇◇	＞＞ ＞＞
319	**367**	**368**	**369**

◼◼ ◼◼	◆◆ ◆◆	◖◖ ◖◖	⟋⟋ ⟋⟋
500	**991**	**992**	**794**

⊗⊗ ⊗⊗	✚✚ ✚✚
793	**791**

Sage

Salvia officinalis

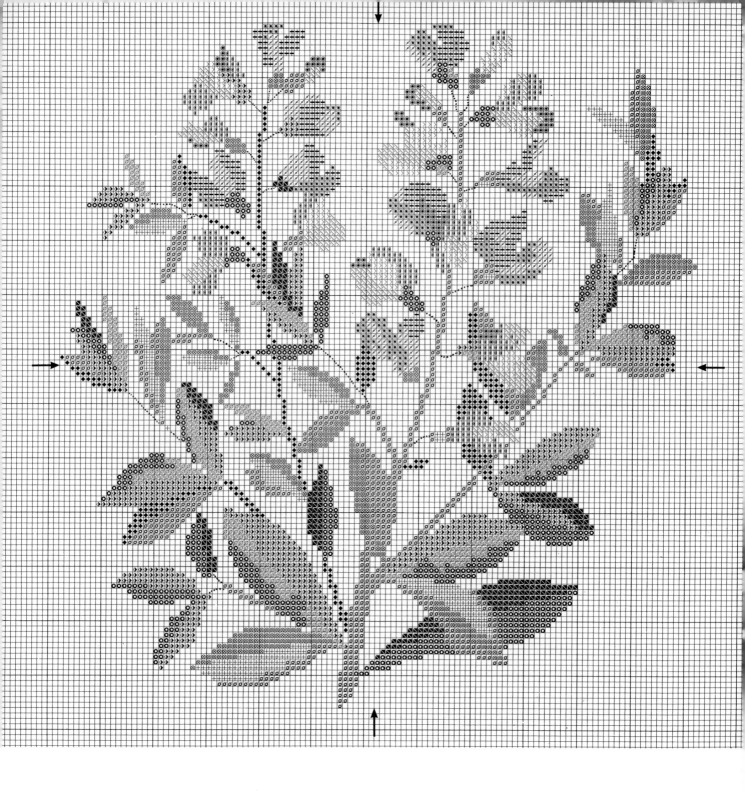

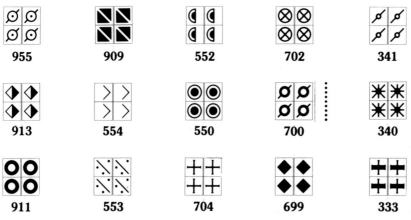

955   909   552   702   341

913   554   550   700   340

911   553   704   699   333

Podalyria

Podalyria australis

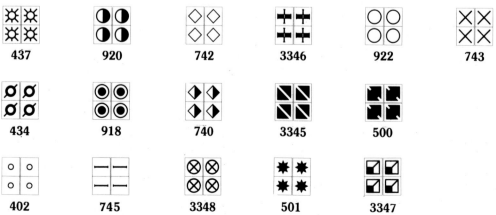

437	920	742	3346	922	743
434	918	740	3345	500	
402	745	3348	501	3347	

Tithonia rotundifolia

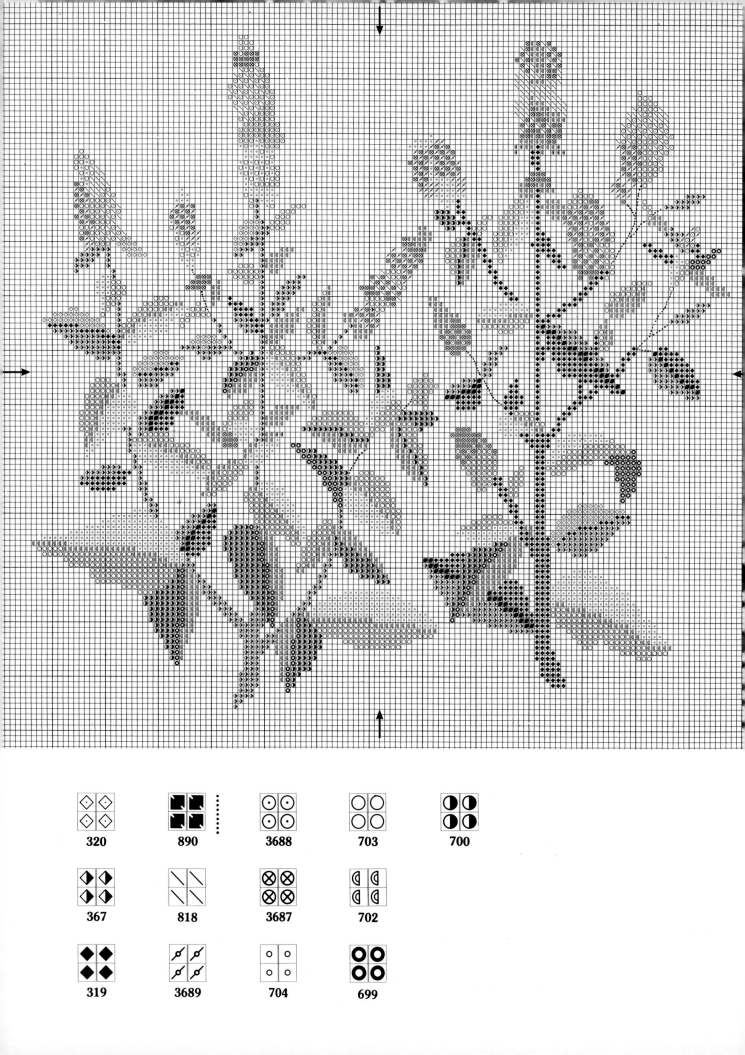

320 890 3688 703 700

367 818 3687 702

319 3689 704 699

Mint

Mentha piperita

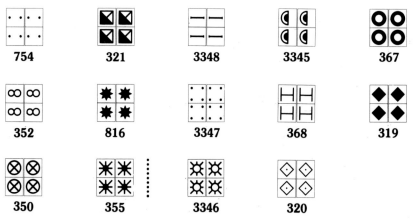

754   321   3348   3345   367

352   816   3347   368   319

350   355   3346   320

Camellia

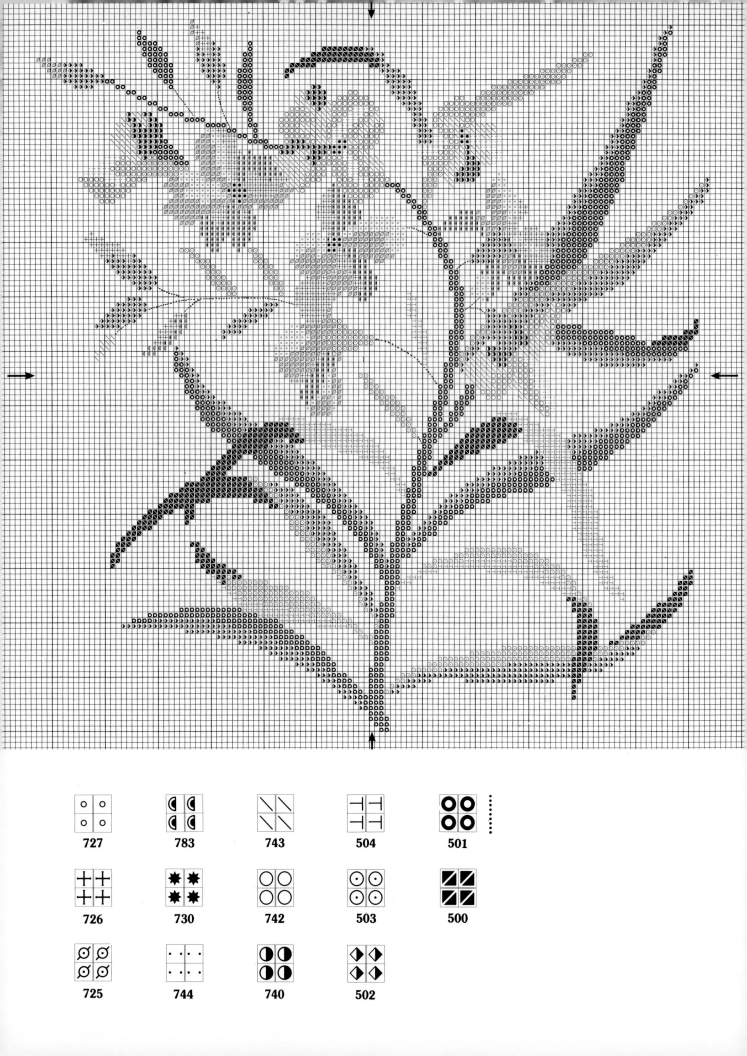

727   783   743   504   501

726   730   742   503   500

725   744   740   502

Stock

Cheizanthus flavus

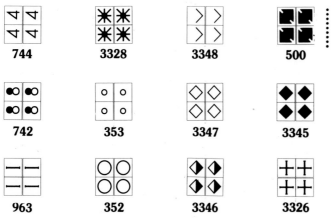

744	**3328**	**3348**	**500**
742	**353**	**3347**	**3345**
963	**352**	**3346**	**3326**

Geranium

Geranium robertianum

918   347   335   3326   3608   blanc white weiß wit

3012   3013   3011   818   3609

369   553   554   320   319

Fuchsia

Fuchsia coccinea

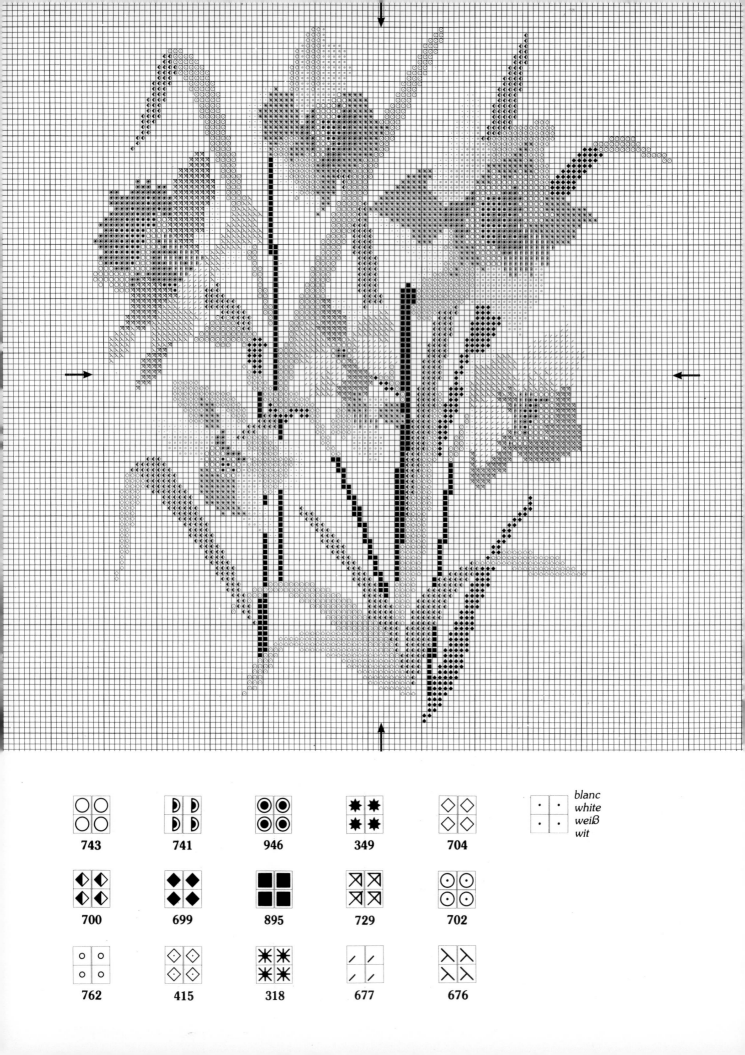

743   741   946   349   704

700   699   895   729   702

762   415   318   677   676

blanc
white
weiß
wit

Narcissus cyclamineus

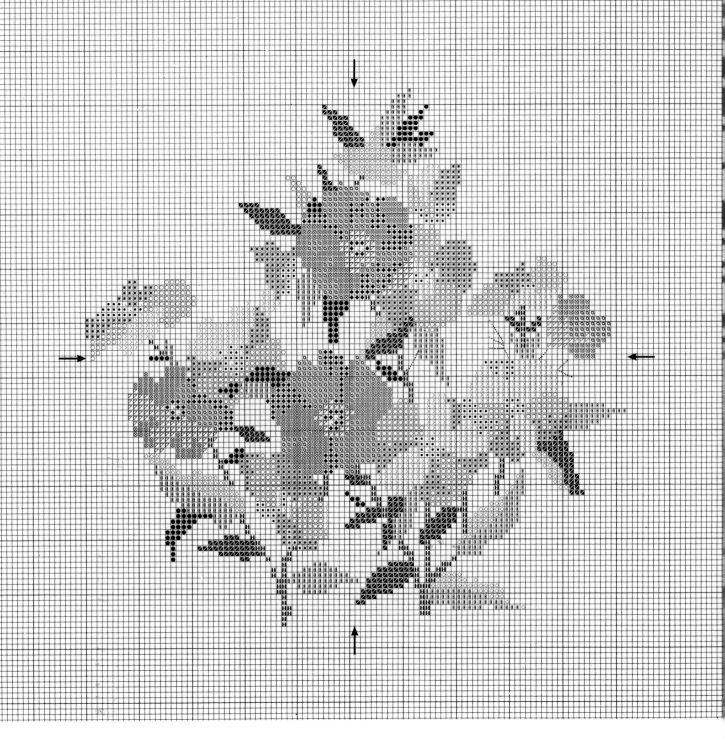

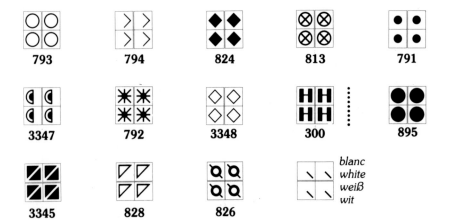

793   794   824   813   791

3347   792   3348   300   895

3345   828   826

blanc
white
weiß
wit

Phlox

Phlox subulata

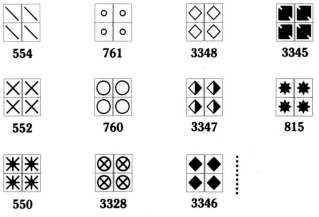

554

761

3348

3345

552

760

3347

815

550

3328

3346

Schizantus

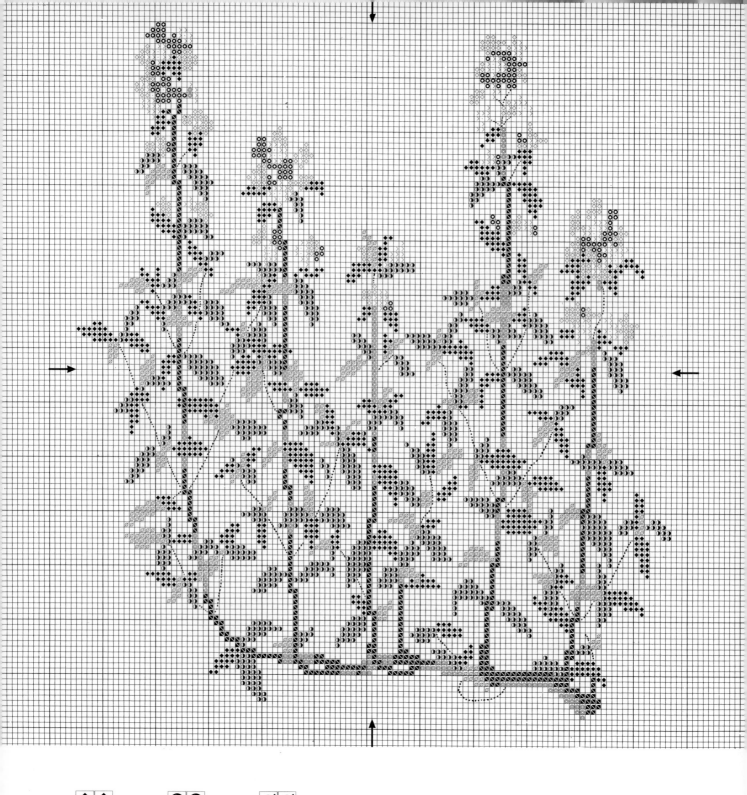

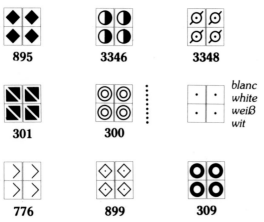

895

3346

3348

301

300

blanc
white
weiß
wit

776

899

309

Wild thyme

Thymum serpyllum

367	743	700	702
319	347	920	704
761	3328	760	890

Primula

Primula sinensis

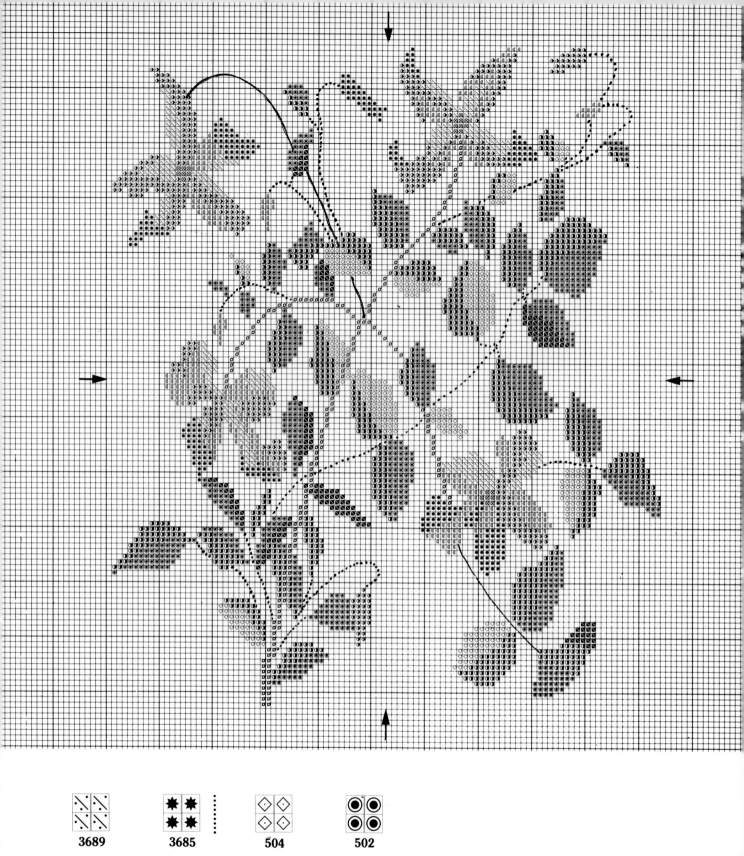

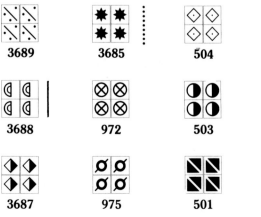

3689

3685

504

502

3688

972

503

3687

975

501

Clematis

Clematis hybrida

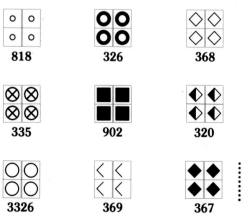

818   326   368   890

335   902   320

3326   369   367

Phlox

Phlox drummondii

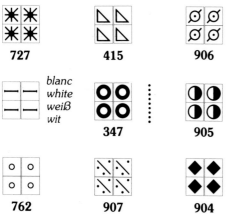

727

415

906

blanc
white
weiß
wit

347

905

762

907

904

Spiraea

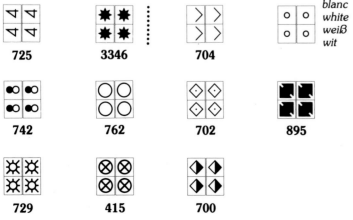

725

3346

704

742

762

702

895

729

415

700

blanc
white
weiß
wit

Feverfew

Chrysanthemum parthenium

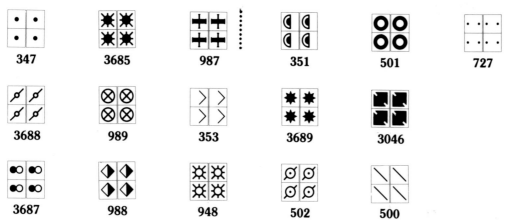

347	3685	987	351	501	727
3688	989	353	3689	3046	
3687	988	948	502	500	

Oleander

Nerium oleander

955	368	828	794	791	824
954	367	813	793	434	742
912	890	820	792	898	911

Phacelia

Phacelia campanularia

Table of contents